MW01387830

CHAMPION SPORT

BIOGRAPHIES

VENUS & SERENA WILLIAMS

CHAMPION SPORT

BIOGRAPHIES

VENUS & SERENA WILLIAMS

KEN SPARLING

W

Warwick Publishing Inc.

Toronto Chicago

www.warwickgp.com

Champion Sport Biographies: Venus & Serena Williams

© 2000 Maverick Communications

All rights reserved. No part of this book may be reproduced, stored in a retrieval system or data base, or transmitted in any form or by any means, electronic, mechanical, photocopying, recording, or otherwise, without the prior written permission of the publisher.

We acknowledge the financial support of the Government of Canada through the Book Publishing Industry Development Program for our publishing activities.

ISBN 1-894020-72-3

Published by Warwick Publishing Inc.
162 John Street
Toronto, Ontario M5V 2E5 Canada
www.warwickgp.com

Distributed in the United States by:
LPC Group
1436 West Randolph Street
Chicago, Illinois
60607

Distributed in Canada by:
General Distribution Services Ltd.
325 Humber College Blvd.
Toronto, ON
M9W 7C3

Design: Heidi Gemmill
Editor: Annis Karpenko
Series Editor: Joseph Romain

Cover and interior photos courtesy of AP/Wide World Photos

Printed and bound in Canada

Table of Contents

Factsheet

Venus Ebone Starr Williams

Born: Lynwood, California

Birthday: June 17, 1980

Residence: Florida

Height: 6 ft. 1 in. (185.5 cm)

Weight: 167 lbs. (76 kg)

Plays: Right-handed (two-handed backhand)

Career Titles (as of December 1999): 7

Favorite color: Silver

Favorite author: J.R.R. Tolkien

Hobbies: surfing, jet skiing, playing guitar, shopping

Serena Williams

Born: Saginaw, Michigan

Birthday: Sept 26, 1981

Residence: Florida

Height: 5 ft. 10 in. (178 cm)

Weight: 145 lbs. (66 kg)

Plays: Right-handed (two-handed backhand)

Career Titles (as of December 1999): 4

Favorite color: Purple

Favorite author: Maya Angelou

Hobbies: surfing, skateboarding, inline skating

Introduction

Welcome to the Williams Show

Halfway through the 1997 U.S. Open semi-final match between Venus Williams and Irina Spirlea, the two players switched ends on the court. This is standard procedure in tennis; players change at every odd-numbered game. What wasn't standard procedure was the bump Spirlea gave Venus as they passed each other at the net.

Spirlea claimed she bumped Venus because she didn't like her attitude. She told reporters she found Venus to be arrogant. Spirlea may have been frustrated by the fact that she, a seven-year veteran and a top-ranked player, was having trouble handling the number 66–ranked player. But Spirlea was not the first, nor would she be the last women's tennis professional to complain about Venus's attitude.

Venus was 17 years old when she arrived at the U.S. Open in 1997. She had been playing professional tennis for three years, since she was just 14 years old. On this Sunday afternoon in September of 1997, Venus was being watched on televisions the world over. Her hair was done up in hundreds of tiny little beads, just like always. Her muscular body was clothed in a tennis outfit that her sports clothing sponsor, Reebok, was paying her to wear.

When a tennis player wins the U.S. Open Tennis Tournament for the first time, she makes hundreds of thousands of dollars and becomes a star. If Venus Williams lost this tournament, she would make hundreds of thousands of dollars anyway, and just getting to the finals had already made her a star.

By the time Spirlea bumped her, Venus had already won the first of the best-of-three sets in the match. Venus wasn't supposed to be doing this well. She was unseeded at the tournament. The top players at any professional tennis tournament are ranked according to their past record, and Venus was not ranked at all for the U.S. Open. No one ever expected to see her in the finals. Certainly, she should not have been beating Spirlea.

Spirlea went on to win the second set, 6-4. At this point the audience might have been excused for believing Venus's chance for winning was over. It really looked like Venus had just got lucky in the first set.

It took a grueling 2 hours and 42 minutes to finish the match. Toward the end, the score in the third set was 7-6. To win a set a player must be up by two games, so this meant Venus and Spirlea had to play a tiebreaker. Spirlea was one point away from winning the match, not once, but twice during the tiebreaker. Both times Spirlea made great shots that many players might have given up on. But not Venus. Venus fought back.

When Venus had clawed her way back to within one point of winning, Spirlea hit a shot that looked like a sure thing — no one in the audience thought Venus could get to the ball. She was out of position as the ball came up the sideline.

Not only did Venus manage to get to the ball, she got off a backhand shot that Spirlea could not touch; all she could do was watch as it touched down on the sideline. Venus had won the semi-finals of the U.S. Open. She was only the second unseeded female tennis player in history to make it to the finals of the U.S. Open.

This was big news. But it seemed for a time that the bump Spirlea gave Venus was even bigger news. Venus's father and coach, Richard Williams, claimed that Spirlea's bump was racially motivated, that Spirlea had plowed into Venus because Venus is black. Richard called Spirlea "that big, white turkey," in a quote that the press was quick to pick up on. Richard later retracted his accusations about racism.

Spirlea admitted later that she bumped Venus intentionally, but insisted that it had nothing to do with race. She refused to apologize for the incident. She showed no remorse, either, for the post-game profanities she used in describing Venus Williams to the press. Ultimately, tennis officials reviewed the incident and fined Spirlea $5,000 for making inappropriate remarks.

Venus wound up losing the 1997 U.S. Open finals to Martina Hingis, the No. 1 ranked women's tennis player in the world, but it didn't matter. She had made her mark. It was clear that she would be a contender.

* * *

Two years later, the Williams family was back at Arthur Ashe Stadium to watch their daughter play in the finals of the 1999 U.S. Open. This time however, it wasn't Venus who was playing, it was her younger sister, Serena.

Unlike Venus, who two years earlier was unseeded coming into the 1997 U.S. Open, Serena was considered one of the top players at the tournament in 1999. She was seeded seventh, meaning she was considered the seventh best player at the tournament.

In order to get to the finals, Serena had beaten some of the top-ranked players in women's tennis. She beat No. 4 seed Monica Seles and the No. 2 ranked player in the world, Lindsay Davenport. In order to take the final, she would have to beat the woman who had stopped Venus's run for the U.S. Open two years earlier — Martina Hingis, the top-ranked women's tennis player in the world.

Hingis had made it to the finals of the 1999 U.S. Open by beating Venus in the semi-finals. If she thought she had got past the tougher of the two Williams sisters, she was in for a surprise. Twice in the past, Hingis had had to play both the Williams girls at a single tournament, and both times she wound up losing to one of the sisters.

Hingis has said that she felt like she was behind the whole time she was playing Serena at the U.S. Open, scrambling to keep up. And scramble she did.

Serena took the first set easily, 6-3. The second set was not so easy. Serena was ahead again, 5-3, and it looked like she was going to go all the way, when her luck turned. Twice she was a point away from winning, and twice she blew it. Hingis managed to come back and take the next game. Serena, however, was still only one game away from victory.

Serena served the next game and again, she played to within a single point of winning. Again she blew it, slamming a forehand out of bounds.

After that, Hingis managed to claw her way back and actually pull ahead 6-5. Serena came back and forced the set into a tiebreaker.

After the tournament, Serena said that that was when she relaxed and took control.

"I feel I can't lose in tiebreakers," she said. "That's when the serve really counts."

She had good reason to be confident. Of the five previous tiebreakers she had played in 1999, she had not lost one.

The tiebreaker was at 4-4 when Serena hit an untouchable forehand to make it 5-4 in her favor. In the next rally, Hingis lobbed one over Serena's head. Serena chased hard but couldn't get to it. Just when she had given up, the ball touched down out of bounds.

On the next rally, Hingis hit a backhand long. Serena dropped down to her knees, clutched at her heart and mouthed the words, *"Oh, my God, I won, oh my God."*

She had taken the U.S. Open, beating world No. 1 Martina Hingis.

* * *

Between the time Venus made it to the finals of the U.S. Open in 1997, and the time Serena won the 1999 U.S. Open, the two girls had risen meteorically through the ranks of the Women's Tennis Association, which includes hundreds of professional players from all around the world.

Between them, the Williams sisters had won more than a dozen titles, many of them in the U.S., but others in places like Italy, Germany, Switzerland, and France. By the end of 1999, Venus and Serena were ranked, respectively, No. 3 and No. 4 in the world. There was no good reason to believe that they wouldn't be able to fulfill their father's prophecy and one day become No. 1 and No. 2. Which of the sisters would be No. 1 and which No. 2 remained to be seen.

But the story of the Williams sisters starts long before either Venus or Serena began competing at a professional level. It begins before either of the girls was born. It begins, in fact, not with Venus and Serena at all, but with their father, Richard Williams, who one fateful day saw a woman's tennis tournament on TV.

Chapter One

Daddy's Little Girls

Richard Williams was born in Shreveport, Louisiana, where his mother, Julia Mae Williams, brought him up. His mother supported Richard and his four sisters by doing common labor, jobs like picking cotton.

After he finished high school, Richard moved to Los Angeles where he soon met Oracene Price, his future wife. While he was in Los Angeles, he went to college and to Los Angeles City School of Business.

Oracene, whose father worked in a car factory and whose mother was a homemaker, graduated from Eastern Michigan University with degrees in education and nursing.

According to reporters who have interviewed Richard Williams, it is often difficult to know whether or not to believe the things he says. He often makes outrageous claims and he seems to like to exaggerate.

In the early 1990s, Richard began telling people about two of his daughters, Venus and Serena. Richard was claiming his young girls were incredible talents, destined to do great things. Now, it is not unusual for a father to brag — to tell everyone how talented, intelligent, even brilliant his children are. Parents like to believe their kids are outstanding, and Richard Williams was no different. He wanted people to believe that his two youngest daughters were going to be superstars.

Venus and Serena Williams played tennis, and if you listened to Richard, they were good — very good. Richard liked to tell people that his two youngest daughters were going to be the best two women's tennis players in the world one day.

For many years, the story has circulated that Richard taught his daughters tennis so the family could get rich and escape from the ghettos. In 1998, he told *Newsweek* magazine about a tennis tournament he saw on TV many years earlier:

"I saw this person win all this money. I went to my wife and said, 'Let's have kids and make them tennis players.'"

But later in 1998, he told *Women's Sports and Fitness* magazine that he never needed the money his girls have made playing tennis.

"Most people thought we were living in Compton because we couldn't do any better," Richard said. "We were making tons of money. Everyone thought we were poor, that tennis was our way out. It was not."

Richard and his wife Oracene had five children,

all daughters. Although Richard himself was no tennis player (he learned the game by watching videos and reading books), he taught his entire family to play tennis.

Richard's oldest daughters, Yetunde, who now works in a hospital and has studied to be a doctor, Isha, who studied law, and Lyndrea, the middle child, did not take to tennis the way the youngest two, Venus and Serena, did.

Venus Williams was born June 17, 1980, in Lynwood, California. Her sister, Serena, was born 15 months later on September 26, 1981, in Saginaw, Michigan.

In 1983, Richard moved his family to Los Angeles. They lived in a neighborhood called Compton, which was well known for its gangs and violence.

Richard first took Venus to the neighborhood tennis courts when she was five. He gave her a racket and started throwing tennis balls over the net. Venus hit the balls back — all 500 of them. In fact, when Richard stopped throwing the balls, Venus cried for more.

The tennis courts in Compton were nothing like the well-maintained courts in the wealthy areas of California where many American tennis pros get their start. The courts the Williams sisters played on were in disrepair. They were falling apart, littered with debris and broken glass, often slippery, even dangerous.

Both Venus and Serena had talent, but more than

that, they were focused on winning, straining with concentration as they played, battering the ball like they were engaged in a war.

War was a way of life for many in the part of Los Angeles where the girls practiced. The tennis courts were in an area where gangs of teenagers often battled, and tennis balls weren't the only things that flew. Sometimes bullets flew as well. Richard Williams likes to tell people that the first thing he taught his daughters when they got onto the tennis courts was how to duck and roll to escape gunfire.

It wasn't long until word got around the neighborhood that Venus and Serena were special. Richard managed to befriend some of the gang members so that when his daughters were on the courts the gangs were generally quiet.

The Williams sisters continued to practice and, just as their father had predicted, they got good. Although the girls have, at times, had some help from professional tennis coaches, throughout much of their career they have relied on their father and mother to coach them.

As it became apparent that Venus and Serena were, indeed, two very special tennis players, Richard Williams was criticized for failing to get his daughters professional coaching. Richard claimed he knew what was best for his children.

His failure to hand his daughters over to professional coaches wasn't the only thing Richard was criticized for. He was also condemned for keeping Venus and Serena off the junior women's circuit, which is generally the breeding ground for professionals.

Venus actually did play in junior competition for a brief period of time. When she was 10 years old, she was unbeaten on the Southern California junior circuit, winning 30 titles and becoming the No. 1 ranked player. It was at this time that Venus and Serena were beginning to draw the attention of people in the tennis world. The two girls were invited to play at a "Just Say No to Drugs" benefit put on by Nancy Reagan, wife of U.S. President Ronald Reagan.

In 1991 the Williams family moved to Florida where the girls enrolled in a well-known tennis school run by Rick Macci. At the same time, Richard took Venus out of junior competition. That's when the criticism really started.

To many, it seemed inconceivable that Venus and Serena would be able to succeed without the tournament experience the juniors provided. Most successful tennis players had played in the juniors, some for many years. Men's tennis greats Andre Agassi and Pete Sampras had both played on the same junior circuit Venus played on briefly in 1989.

But the juniors are also a place where children encounter immense pressure. Playing in the juniors can be difficult and emotionally destructive. There are rumors that some players have suffered emotional problems due to the intense competition of the juniors.

Richard decided to keep his daughters out of the juniors because, as he put it, he had seen, "enough freak shows — kids throwing tantrums, parents yelling at kids, parents fighting other parents."

Some defended Richard's decision. Zina Garrison, who played women's professional tennis for 16 years, once said, "A lot of people were doubting and trying to figure out if what Richard was doing was the right way. I think they should applaud him for believing in what he believed. I think a lot of times you have to go with what you think is best for your child."

Many tennis players turn professional around the time they are 14, sometimes even earlier. A player is considered professional as soon as she has played in one of the many tournaments organized by the Women's Tennis Association, a group that represents women tennis professionals from around the world.

In 1994, around the time Venus was thinking about turning professional, another young player, Jennifer Capriati, was arrested for possession of marijuana.

"It was like the Jennifer thing painted a picture for me," Richard said afterward. He was particularly worried because of the similarities between Capriati's situation and that of Venus.

Capriati had turned professional at age 13. The launch of her professional career had been met with great fanfare in the media, and Capriati had succeeded brilliantly in her first few years on the professional circuit.

By the time she was 14 Capriati was a millionaire. A year later, she was ranked No. 6 in the world. But two years later she was out of the game completely, and she was getting treatment for drug problems when she was 18.

Richard Williams was not willing to risk seeing this happen to his daughter Venus, who was on the verge of a huge media launch herself, and would likely experience the same kind of financial and professional success as Capriati.

"The next time a 14-year-old girl turns pro," Richard proclaimed in his usual blunt manner, "they ought to shoot the parents, hang the coach and send the whole WTA [Women's Tennis Association] staff into exile in the Russian Army."

Richard's desire to protect his daughters seemed sensible, even noble. It might be argued that he was giving a lot up, keeping his girls off the professional circuit. After planning for decades to turn his daughters into tennis stars so they could make a lot of money, Richard was delaying his dream to protect his girls.

There were some people, however, who thought Richard was making a big mistake. Rick Macci, who was coaching Venus and had also coached Jennifer

Capriati, claimed that throwing Venus into the professional fray all at once when she was older would be like having her drive in "the Indy 500 the day after she gets her driver's license."

Venus wound up turning professional at the age of 14, only a few months after Richard had vowed to the media that he would keep her out of competition until she was 16. It was headstrong Venus who made the decision to go pro. After Richard announced that Venus would be playing in a professional tournament in Oakland, California on October 31, 1994, he went on to say, "I'm completely against it. I think it's insane." He told members of the press that it had been Venus's decision entirely.

When asked how soon it would be before Venus signed with an agent and started playing a lot of tournaments, Richard refused to comment. "I've already made a fool out of myself once," he told reporters.

Even after Venus turned professional at the end of 1994, followed by her sister a year or so later, Richard insisted they limit the number of tournaments they played in. This was partly so they wouldn't burn out, partly so they could continue their education. Richard and Oracene were determined to make sure their daughters didn't turn into two-dimensional tennis players with no life off the courts.

For the most part, the girls themselves seemed quite happy to go along with Richard's program of limited tournament play. Even as late as 1999, Serena was limiting the number of tournaments she played in. When asked in an interview if she would be playing in more than 20 tournaments in 1999, she answered, "No. Gees, no. That's just out of control. I don't agree with that . . . I'm going to school later on this year, to college."

Richard wanted his girls to survive, not just during their years as tennis pros, but beyond. So, the girls stayed in school and entered the world of professional tennis gradually.

To some, Venus and Serena's parents seemed overprotective. The girls' mother, Oracene, never even allowed baby-sitters to look after her children. She stayed home when her daughters were young so they wouldn't have to go to pre-school. When the family moved to Florida, Richard and Oracene homeschooled their youngest daughters.

Of course, Venus and Serena would eventually have to go out into the world of professional tennis if they were going to make their mark. But they would do it on their own terms and in their own time.

Chapter Two

The Williams Girls Go Pro

In the fall of 1994, 21-year-old Arantxa Sanchez Vicario was the second-best women's tennis player in the world. She had won her first Grand Slam event, the French Open, at the precocious age of 17. She was an Olympic medallist and was destined to become the number one women's tennis player in the world only a year later.

Venus Williams was 14 years old and was playing in her first professional tournament when she met Sanchez Vicario on the tennis courts in Oakland, California, at the end of 1994.

Venus became a professional tennis player at an age when most kids are just trying to sort out who they are and what they are going to do with their lives. Unlike most kids, Venus not only knew what she wanted to do with her life, she was already doing it.

For most people, it takes time to become accustomed to a new career. Some call it a "learning curve," a period of time during which a person learns to adapt to new surroundings. If her first tournament was any indication, Venus Williams seemed to need no time at all to adapt. She won the very first match of her professional career, easily beating the No. 59 player in the world, Shaun Stafford, 6-3, 6-4. This put her into the second round where she would be playing Arantxa Sanchez Vicario.

Women's professional tennis tournaments are played on a round robin basis. A player who wins a match moves on to the next round. To win a match, a player must win the best of three sets. The player who first wins six games wins a set.

The match between Venus and Sanchez Vicario should have been no contest. Sanchez Vicario should have won easily. Venus was still just a kid and a newcomer to professional tennis. Sanchez Vicario was a mature woman and a seasoned professional.

So it was a big shock to the tennis world when young Venus Williams beat the seasoned Sanchez Vicario 6-3 in the first set of their match. Then in the second set, Venus won the first three games. Finally, Arantxa seemed to get her act together. She managed a comeback to beat Venus, eventually winning the match.

To dominate the opening games in a match against someone as formidable as Arantxa Sanchez Vicario was an incredible feat for a girl just barely into high school, a girl playing only the second match of her professional career.

Every tennis player is given a certain number of

points each time she does well in a tournament. The total number of points a player accumulates determines where they are ranked in relation to all the other players on the circuit. There are hundreds and hundreds of players on the circuit, all struggling to be number one. It takes a consistently good performance week after week, tournament after tournament, to climb in rankings.

After her stunning debut, Venus might have moved up quickly in the rankings had she played in a lot of tournaments. But her father Richard, who also acted as her coach, insisted that she play only a very limited schedule that first year.

Two years after her professional debut, at the age of 16, Venus had played in less than a dozen tournaments. In what was only her tenth professional tournament, she again rocked the tennis world by beating No. 9 player Iva Majoli in the quarterfinals of a tournament at Indian Wells, California.

After beating Majoli, Venus went on to the semifinals at Indian Wells. There she pushed No. 8 Lindsay Davenport to a third-set tiebreaker before losing 6-4, 5-7, 7-6. Venus hadn't won, but she'd made Davenport sweat, and that was an achievement in itself. Davenport was an extremely powerful player who would climb to the No. 1 spot in women's tennis rankings in the next few years,.

On the strength of her performance at Indian Wells,

Venus jumped more than a hundred points in the rankings, from No. 211 to No. 110. She also reached the doubles quarterfinals at Indian Wells with her sister Serena.

But Venus's success was short-lived. She began to show poor results. When this happened, the critics were right there, ready to pounce. They claimed that they had been right all along, that Venus's success had been a fluke. Although Venus had had a brief flash of success, they opined, she was far from championship material.

Venus went to a fuller schedule of tournaments in 1997. She didn't do too badly at a tournament early in the season called the Lipton Championship, which is considered one of the top five events of the women's professional tennis year.

She got off to a rocky start, losing five games to No. 28 Jennifer Capriati, who had returned to tennis and was trying to rebuild her career after her emotional setbacks. But then Venus managed to get back in the game, and eventually defeated Capriati. She would lose in the third round to Martina Hingis. But still, beating Capriati was a triumph.

After the Lipton Championship, however, things did not go well. Venus began to lose a lot. Criticism grew, not just of her abilities, but of the arrogant confidence both she and her father seemed to have, even when faced with the facts. And the facts at that point were not very encouraging.

It seems, however, that a measure of arrogance, or what looks like arrogance, might be a necessary character trait in someone who wants to succeed in the world of professional tennis. In fact, some might claim that what Venus and Richard Williams showed was not arrogance at all, but rather confidence, a confidence needed to win in a highly competitive field.

In the world of professional tennis, the real champions are measured by their performance at the four Grand Slam tournaments. The Grand Slams are four very special events that every player wants to win. They are the Australian Open, the French Open, Wimbledon (played in England), and the United States Open.

In 1997, Venus did not do well at the first of the Grand Slam events, the Australian Open. Nor did she do well at the French Open, where she lost in the second round. And at Wimbledon, at the beginning of the summer, she did even worse, losing in the first round.

But if many people were criticizing Venus, and others were writing her off as a flash in the pan — someone who dazzled the tennis world briefly and then fizzled out — she herself wasn't giving up.

The final Grand Slam event each year is the U.S. Open. Venus showed what was becoming her usual poor performance in the first round of the tournament, losing the first set she played against a player named Larissa Neiland.

But if Venus's game still needed improving, her determination to win did not. She came back to beat Neiland in the next two sets to win the match. She didn't lose another set in the tournament until she hit the semi-finals. She beat No. 8 Anke Huber. She beat Sandrine Testud. The semi-final match against No. 11 Irina Spirlea was a real thriller, with two of the sets going to tiebreakers.

Remember, in order to win a set of tennis, a player must be ahead by two games. When two players are equally matched, they might trade wins back and forth for hours, with neither player getting ahead by more than a single game. To keep tennis matches from going for too long, when a set goes beyond six games with neither player ahead by two, a sudden death game called a tiebreaker is played.

In her first set against Spirlea, Venus won the tiebreaker. But then she lost the second set, 4-6. The third set went, again, to a tiebreaker. Toward the end of the tiebreaker, Spirlea needed a single point for the win. She hit a shot down the sideline, catching Venus out of position. No one watching the match thought Venus could get to the ball, least of all Spirlea. Miraculously, Venus not only got to the ball, but when she did, she hit a devastating backhand shot that got past Spirlea and just touched down on the sideline.

Venus eventually won the match, becoming only the

second unseeded player in history to make it to the finals of the U.S. Open.

It was during the 1997 U.S. Open semi-final match between Venus and Spirlea that the now famous bumping incident occurred. Spirlea bumped Venus intentionally when the girls were changing ends on the court. Spirlea also swore at Venus during a press conference and was fined for doing so.

In an interview with *Tennis* magazine, Spirlea admitted she was playing a game of chicken when she bumped into Williams. "I wanted to see if she would step aside." At that point, Venus was developing a reputation, not only as a great tennis player, but also as an arrogant one.

Spirlea wasn't the only player to complain about Venus. Brenda Schultz-McCarthy said that Venus once greeted her at the net after a match by saying, "Don't touch me!" When reporters asked Venus about this, she responded, "I don't hold great conversations. Actually, I don't hold conversations at all."

At the same press conference, Venus said she thought that her presence on the WTA circuit could save women's tennis. When asked if she admired any of the other players on the circuit, she answered, "No, I don't."

Anne Miller had a story to tell as well. In the first round of the tournament in Indian Wells in 1997, Venus beat Miller. When the two met at the net to shake hands, Venus told Miller, "You beat my sister. I owed you."

Lindsay Davenport, Monica Seles, and Jennifer Capriati all tell stories about Venus ignoring them when they said hi or smiled at her when they met by chance off the courts.

Williams is surprised when people call her arrogant. "Why don't you guys tell me what they want me to do?" she said to reporters at one point. "They should come up to me and say, 'Venus, I want you to smile so I can feel better.' When I want to smile, I'll smile. If I don't want to, I'm not going to. I think it's a little bit peevish. Smiling — what does that have to do with anything?"

Venus has never denied she is different from most women on the tennis circuit. She once told *Newsweek* magazine that "most of the past tennis stars have been all-American or -European who've been lovable. Me and Serena are a whole different thing happening."

Having two African Americans at center court in women's tennis, especially two so talented as the Williams sisters, cannot help but be a source of inspiration to others.

"So many minorities think there's only basketball and football," says NBA teen heart-throb Kobe Bryant. "Now they have these girls doing their thing. I stay glued to the TV when they're playing."

Richard Williams has indicated that he believes the

white-dominated world of tennis to be capable of racism. But he has other reasons for disapproving of some people in professional tennis. When he quit accompanying his daughters to their tournaments, he pointed out that Venus and Serena didn't need him out there any more. He had his own life, he said, a life more worthwhile than some parents of tennis stars who travel everywhere with their children.

He also didn't seem much interested in the sport itself. Just before Wimbledon in 1997, Richard told reporters, "You sit there, with your head going this way and that way, clapping like a seal at the zoo, and I'm tired of that. I've been doing that since [Venus] was four years old. I want my head to stand still some."

After the 1998 U.S. Open, Richard told Kevin Chappell of *Ebony* magazine that he wished Venus would "get the hell out of New York and get back to pursuing her education . . . I would like to see her get out of tennis completely." Richard claimed that "professional tennis is guilty of blinding young women with fame and money."

Despite their father's qualms, the Williams sisters played on. The other player who made it to the finals of the 1997 U.S. Open was Martina Hingis, who, in the coming years, would become a major rival of Venus and Serena. Venus was unable to defeat Hingis in the U.S. Open finals. But just making it to the finals showed what a great player Venus was.

When Serena entered the professional circuit toward the end of 1997, Venus had not yet won a Grand Slam event. In fact, she had not yet won a tournament. There was much speculation on the part of the media and fans about which of the Williams sisters would first win a tournament and about who would first grab a Slam. Would it be Venus with her blistering serve and constantly improving game? Or would it be little sister Serena with less experience but, according to many, more talent?

Their father Richard once said, "Serena is the best one of the two. What makes me think she will be better is she has had years to sit around and watch Venus . . . She always was a better athlete than Venus to start off with. She hits the ball harder and returns the serve better."

Serena immediately caused a sensation when she joined the professional tennis circuit, partly because she was Venus's sister, but also because she played well. People were eager to see if she could measure up to her father's often outrageous claims about her talent. Venus had certainly been able to live up to Richard Williams's predictions, but could Serena repeat this success?

Serena Williams joined the Women's Tennis Association professional rankings in October of 1997 at No. 453. Within the space of just a few weeks, she moved up to No. 304. Just three weeks after entering the rankings, at the second main event she entered, Serena proved she was better than at least two of the top 10 players in the world. She beat No. 7 Mary Pierce and No. 4 Monica Seles, to make it to the semi-finals of a tournament in Chicago. This brilliant performance saw Serena move up more than 200 places in the rankings to No. 102.

It would be more than a year from the time Serena entered the rankings until she won a Women's Tennis Association singles title. In fact, she would get no higher than the semi-finals in 1998, and then only once, at her first tournament of 1998, the Sydney International.

Venus, on the other hand, would have a considerably more successful year in 1998.

Serena and Venus Williams pose for the cameras in Eastbourne, England, in June 1997 during the Direct Line Ladies Tennis Championsips. Venus was preparing for her first appearance at Wimbledon.

Venus smiles as a fan takes her photo while she signs autographs following her win over Silvija Talaja of Croatia at the Australian Open in January 1999.

Serena celebrates her semi-final win over Number One seed Martina Hingis at the Lipton Championships on March 26, 1999, in Florida.

U.S. team members Serena Williams, Monica Seles, and Venus Williams smile during introductions of the American and Russian teams in the finals of the Fed Cup in California in September 1999.

Chapter Three

The Big Four, 1998

In 1997, Venus had shown that she had raw talent. She had speed. She had power. Still, some critics claimed Venus had made it to the semi-finals of the U.S. Open, not because of her great booming power shots, but in spite of them. If she was going to make it to the top, she was going to have to show that she could do more than hit the ball hard. She would have to learn to think on her feet, to change her game as circumstances changed.

The Women's Tennis Association tour of events includes a tennis tournament just about every week-end of the year, sometimes more than one, so there are about 60 events a year. But the four tournaments that are considered most important, the ones every professional player wants to win, are the Grand Slam events — the Australian Open, held early in the year, the French Open, held in the spring, Wimbledon, held in the early summer, and the U.S. Open, held in early fall.

1998 Australian Open

If Irina Spirlea was glad to put the controversy surrounding her collision with Venus at the 1997 U.S. Open behind her, she must have cringed when she saw who she was playing in the first round of the next Grand Slam event, the 1998 Australian Open. One thing was certain: she was not about to bump this opponent, who just happened to be Venus's sister, Serena.

And if Spirlea thought she might fare better in her game against the younger of the Williams sisters, she had a big surprise in store.

Spirlea was seeded sixth in the Australian Open, meaning she was considered the sixth-best player at the event. Serena, on the other hand, was unseeded. There was no reason to believe she would progress very far in the tournament. It turned out that Serena didn't get all that far, but she did get past Spirlea, which was quite an upset.

Venus also won her first-round match at the Australian Open, setting up a match that was definitely one of the highlights of the tournament: Spectators would be treated to a second-round match between Venus and Serena.

It was the first time the Williams sisters had played one another in a professional match. How would the two girls react? Would Serena hold back in deference to her older sister? Would Venus show any protective instincts for the baby of the Williams family? How would the girls feel about one another after the match was over and only one of them moved on to the next round of the Australian Open?

These were the kinds of questions on everybody's minds as Venus and Serena faced each other over the net in Melbourne, Australia, in January of 1998.

It would be only the seventh time in tennis history that sisters had competed against one another in a Grand Slam event. If past experience had any bearing, Venus had the advantage. Every time sisters had played against each other in a Grand Slam match in the past, the older sister had won.

Tennis experts had been speculating about which of the Williams sisters would dominate women's tennis in the new millennium. Now people would get a little taste of things to come.

At every tennis tournament, there are a number of different tennis courts where games are played. The most important games — those involving top-seeded players — are played at center court. Many of the early matches in a tournament are played on less prominent courts.

The match between Venus and Serena was played on center court on the third day of the tournament. It was something special for two unseeded players.

"The first time they ever played each other was in a tournament in Indian Wells, when we were living in

California," their mother Oracene pointed out to reporters in Australia. "Serena wasn't supposed to be in it, but she entered herself, filled out all the forms and everything. She was eight years old. She said she was in the tournament, and I said, 'No, you're not,' and she told me to check with the organizers. There she was, entered. Serena wound up losing to Venus in the final."

At the 1998 Australia Open, Serena lost again. It was not a particularly close match, but there was no doubt that both girls gave it everything they had.

Success in professional tennis, as in any sport, comes down to the athlete's ability to focus. The key to becoming a champion, if you listen to the experts, is concentration. A true champion will focus all her attention on the play at hand. She won't think about who she is playing, or what the current score is. She thinks about nothing but where the ball is, where it is going, and what she needs to do to stop the other player from winning the point.

Venus and Serena had been working on developing this sort of concentration for a long time. What's more, they had been playing against each other since they were toddlers. It is not so surprising that both girls got down to the business of playing and didn't let family get in the way of putting on a great display of tennis.

The crowd who witnessed the historic event in Australia gave their biggest applause when the two sisters met after the match. Venus hugged Serena and then the two bowed to the audience, hands clasped tightly together.

As history would have it, it was not long before Serena would be posing a somewhat more serious challenge to her sister.

After the Australian Open was over, Venus and Serena talked to reporters from *Sports Illustrated* magazine about the tournament. They talked about what it was like to play against each other, of course, but they also talked about other things. They were eager to discuss their favorite music groups: Rancid, Hole, Green Day, and Bad Religion. They talked about jewelry and clothes and of course, the topic all teenage girls like to discuss, boys.

Venus claimed that men's professional tennis player Patrick Rafter lost the third round of the Australian Open mainly because he was wearing a black shirt that neither Venus nor Serena thought he looked good in.

Serena said that on her top 10 list of men's tennis players, Pete Sampras was number one and that he would always be able to beat her at tennis no matter how good she got.

When they finally got down to talking tennis, Venus said, "It wasn't fun eliminating my little sister, but I have to be tough. After the match, I said, 'I'm sorry I had to take you out.'"

Venus pointed out that beating Serena is difficult

because the two practice together so often. They know each other's tricks.

"Serena hates to lose and her reputation is she doesn't lose to anyone twice, so I'm going to be practicing secretly if I want to win the next one," Venus said.

Serena was philosophical: "If I had to lose in the second round, there's no one better to lose to than Venus."

Above all, in Australia Venus and Serena showed that they like to have fun.

After Serena lost, she went out and talked men's professional Karsten Braasch, a 30-year-old German ranked No. 226 in the world, into playing a set of tennis against her, just for the heck of it.

"I'm going to take him out," Serena said of Braasch.

Venus seemed to be jealous of her sister's freedom, now that Serena was out of the tournament. "I am going to play against a man before I leave here," Venus said in a press conference. "I just have to fit it in."

Both girls eventually played Braasch while in Australia. Braasch defeated both soundly.

In the actual tournament, Venus went on to be the only unseeded player to make it to the quarterfinals. In the quarterfinals, she played Lindsay Davenport.

Although much of the media hype concerning women's tennis rivalries has centered on the Williams sisters' battle to overcome Martina Hingis, Lindsay Davenport is also a serious foe. Right up to the end of

1999, Davenport had remained ahead of both Venus and Serena in the rankings, holding onto the No. 2 spot, right behind Hingis. After the 2000 Australian Open, Davenport was, for the second time in her career, threatening to take the number one spot away from Hingis.

Both Venus and Davenport are power players. They are both tall and have wicked serves. They both like to hit the ball hard and deep into their opponent's court. But Davenport had much more experience than Venus.

In the first set of the 1998 Australian Open quarterfinals, Venus out-powered Davenport completely, beating her 6-1. For some players, the psychological disadvantage of losing so badly might have spelled certain doom. But Davenport fought back in a second set that went to seven games, with Davenport winning 7-5. Venus seemed to lose her confidence completely at that point. Davenport won the final set 6-3, taking Venus out of the Australian Open.

Still, Venus had made it to the quarterfinals of a major tournament. She had played well against one of the best women's players in the world. And she now rose in the women's tennis rankings to No. 14.

Although Venus was unable to make it past the quarterfinals in singles play at the Australian Open, her performance in the mixed doubles tournament was another story.

Doubles play in tennis involves two players playing as partners on each side of the net. Mixed doubles means the partners consist of one man and one woman on each team. Venus's partner in 1998 was Justin Gimelstob, and the two of them went all the way at the Australian Open, winning Venus her first Grand Slam trophy. Granted, it was not the singles Grand Slam that every player wants to win, but it was a start.

1998 French Open

Venus came on the scene before her sister, but some believe that Serena will wind up being the stronger player as they each come into their prime. Serena is smaller and stronger, perfect for a good game all around. Venus has the power advantage her height gives her, but she has to work harder to get around in the backcourt.

Serena seems to genuinely enjoy herself on the court. She gets great joy out of her wins and showing real desire when she's down. Venus, on the other hand, sometimes seems less committed to the game. When she lost to Hingis in the quarterfinals of the 1998 French Open, there were reports that Venus seemed strangely unemotional, as though it was no big deal. She might have simply been covering up an intense disappointment.

But there are times when Venus does not seem to

care as much about tennis as her sister. Venus is a powerful athlete and that alone can take a player a long way. But, bottom line, a player must have the will to win.

"I think Venus wants to do other things," her mother Oracene told *Newsweek* magazine in 1998. "She does what's expected of her until it's done."

For someone who claims to want to be the No. 1 women's tennis player in the world, this seems a bit strange. It's like saying she plays tennis for the same reasons she cleans up her room when asked to do so by her parents.

"There are so many things that I want to do that are more creative," says Venus. "Like designing clothes. Not runway fashions or anything like that. I'm more into clothes for average people."

The French Open was the second Grand Slam event in a row that Venus had lost in the quarterfinals. It was also the second clay court tournament in a row where Martina Hingis ousted her. Not a month earlier, Hingis had defeated Venus in the finals of the Italian Open.

Hingis and Venus had met eight times and Hingis had won on six of those occasions. Venus would have to do better if she was going to take over the No. 1 ranking.

Venus's performance in mixed doubles at the French Open was outstanding, and on June 6, 1998, she and

Gimelstob won their second Grand Slam in a row. The pair might have gone on to win the other two Grand Slams in 1998, Wimbledon and the U.S. Open, but sister Serena was to get in the way.

Serena didn't do quite as well at the French Open. She managed to make it to the fourth round in singles play by slaughtering 15th seed Dominique Van Roost, 6-1, 6-1. But in the fourth round she ran up against Arantxa Sanchez Vicario and wound up losing.

1998 Wimbledon

Wimbledon is the most prestigious tennis event of the season. The tournament at Wimbledon has also been around longer than any other event currently on the tennis calendar, having started well over a hundred years ago in the 1880s. In those days, tennis was played on grass. Wimbledon is still played on grass; it is, in fact, the only Grand Slam event still played on a lawn.

The highlight for Venus at Wimbledon occurred in the second round, where she played Barbara Schett. Poor Schett was on the receiving end of a serve that broke all the records. Venus slammed one into Schett's court at 125 mph (201 km/h), 2 mph (3 km/h) faster than the previous record set by Brenda Schultz-McCarthy. Before breaking the record, Venus's fastest had been 122 mph (196 km/h).

"That was a real surprise," Venus said afterwards. "I

wasn't going for any big ones today. I could have served harder. I wasn't even really trying to serve that hard in the match. But I'm trying to add nine mph [14.5 km/h] to my serve each year, so it's nice to see that number."

When Serena heard about her sister's mega-serve, she said, "Jeepers. She's much bigger than I am, she's taller, and she might have more power. I really don't know if I can catch up with that."

Although Venus broke the record for fastest serve and made it to the quarterfinals at Wimbledon, she didn't have a great time there, nor did Serena.

For many years, tennis, and in particular women's tennis, was a very staid and proper English-style affair. The players were very polite. The audience remained quiet so that the players could concentrate.

The game got its start in England among members of the upper class, wealthy people with plenty of leisure time. Upper class people were always very refined. They never threw tantrums or showed a lot of emotion — at least not in public. So tennis remained a very cultivated sport.

All that changed in the 1970s when players like John McEnroe and Boris Becker came on the scene. These players argued with the judges at matches, they threw temper tantrums. and often went so far as to throw their rackets.

During the quarterfinal match with Jana Novotna at

Wimbledon, Venus became frustrated and angry when a series of line calls went against her. No doubt Venus was upset partly because she was struggling to keep up with Novotna. But she may also have been showing some frustration because of the repressive atmosphere at Wimbledon.

Every time the Williams sisters entered the court area during their stay at Wimbledon, the security guard, who knew exactly who they were, asked them for their passes so he could run them through the electric scanners.

"Only scan once a day," Venus told the guard. "I'm not into all that scanning."

Serena was amazed to find out that there was no place to practice at Wimbledon on a Sunday in the middle of the tournament. Everything was closed up. "I just found out that you can't even practice here," Serena said. "That really went right over my head. I would say that's being traditional."

For Serena, the chances of winning Wimbledon were pretty slim in 1998. It was her first year at tennis's premiere event, and Wimbledon is played on grass, a surface the Williams sisters don't have a great deal of experience on.

There was some talk that Serena might surprise some people at Wimbledon. She had made a stunning debut on grass just before coming to Wimbledon at a place in England called Eastbourne. At Eastbourne,

Serena made it to the quarterfinals, a great accomplishment for someone who had never before played on grass courts.

As it turned out, Serena made it only to the third round of singles play at Wimbledon. But she more than made up for it in the mixed doubles competition. Along with her partner, Max Mirnyi, Serena stopped her sister and Justin Gimelstob, capturing her first Grand Slam event. It wouldn't be her last in 1998.

1998 United States Open

The U.S. Open was Venus's best Grand Slam tournament in 1998. She made it to the semi-finals, but lost there to Lindsay Davenport.

If Venus's game against Davenport wasn't all that hot, at least Venus herself was *looking* hot. The outfit she wore was one of seven supplied by her sponsor, Reebok, a company she had signed with not long after turning professional in 1994. The Reebok deal saw Venus earning a reported twelve million dollars over five years.

The outfit she wore in her match against Davenport was red with the back cut out to expose Venus's muscles. Reebok had planned to have Venus wear a different outfit in each round of the U.S. Open. But since Venus never made it to the finals, she didn't get to wear the seventh outfit.

Serena made her mark at the U.S. Open, not in the

singles competition, but in the mixed doubles. She and Max Mirnyi took their second Grand Slam event.

As a player gets older, she may start to lose some of her power, speed, and agility. But she gains experience. An experienced veteran who has played a lot of tournaments will be better at planning her strategy, and may react more strongly under pressure.

In her first few years, Venus showed a definite lack of experience in her mental game. When she fell behind, she began to make mistakes, trying to smash the ball over every time for a winner, instead of waiting for the right opportunity to hit the ball home. In 1998, Venus began to play a more strategic game, and although she didn't manage to win a Grand Slam event, she did win some tournaments.

Serena, too, had had some problems due to her inexperience — perhaps even more problems than her sister. At one tournament, Arantxa Sanchez Vicario almost lost an early match in straight sets to Serena. But then, only two points away from wrapping things up, Serena lost control of the game. Sanchez Vicario began to fight her way back, and Serena got more and more desperate, eventually leveling a shot right at Sanchez Vicario's head.

Serena had another emotional setback in the summer of 1998 at Wimbledon, when she started falling behind Virginia Ruano-Pascual of Spain. Serena actually quit in the middle of the match, during her second set, saying that her leg was hurting her. But the next day, she played mixed doubles and seemed to have no problem with her leg. When questioned by reporters, Serena made no secret of the fact that she could have carried on playing the day before.

In some ways, none of this was so surprising. Venus and Serena were teenagers thrown into a world of pressures most teenagers never come close to, even in their wildest dreams (or most frightening nightmares). Like other teenagers, the Williams sisters giggled and joked together about everything from boys to school to their latest clothes. They may have had more confidence than the average high school girl, but they were, after all, only human.

Chapter Four

Winning Tournaments, Getting Groceries

If you were to ask Venus and Serena, in the spring of 1998, what the greatest moment in their young teenage lives had been, they might have told you about one particular trip to the grocery store.

Besides the four Grand Slam events, the Williams sisters played in a number of other tournaments in 1998. One of these was the 1998 IGA Tennis Classic. In preparation for this tournament, Venus and Serena were invited to participate in a promotional event which involved running through a grocery store and loading up a cart with as many groceries as they could in a specific amount of time. It was much like a TV show the girls loved to watch, "Supermarket Sweep."

The girls' mother, Oracene, told *Vogue* magazine that this promotional event was one of the main reasons the girls decided to play in the IGA Classic.

"It's like realizing a dream," Venus said after loading up her cart. "I always wanted to be on that show. It was more exciting than winning a match. I'm not kidding. It was wonderful."

Serena told Reed, "I can't stop thinking about it. I could do this, like, every day."

Venus's claim that running through a grocery store was more exciting than winning a match came before she had won any titles. Perhaps, once she had gone all the way and won a tournament, she would change her tune.

1998 IGA Tennis Classic

Venus had little trouble progressing to the semi-finals of the 1998 IGA Tennis Classic, which is played in Oklahoma City, Oklahoma. The semi-finals were, however, another story. She would be playing Lindsay Davenport who had completely dominated Venus a month earlier in the quarterfinals of the Australian Open.

Davenport struggled in the first set. She managed ultimately to win, but only after the set went to a tiebreaker. In the second set, Venus dominated completely, beating Davenport 6-2.

Davenport came back in the third set, pulling ahead 3-2. At that point, however, Venus turned on the juice and won the next four games to take the match and move on to the finals where she would play South African Joannette Kruger.

Venus had played in two finals so far in her professional career, including her breath-taking run at the U.S. Open in 1997. But she had yet to win a tournament.

Kruger, who was ranked No. 27 at the time of the IGA Classic, had defeated Serena soundly earlier in the tournament, so perhaps Venus felt she needed to take some revenge. If the rankings were any indication, Venus was definitely the better player, ranked 15 places higher than Kruger was at the time. Whatever her motivation, Venus crushed Kruger, 6-3, 6-2, thereby winning her first-ever WTA tour event. She was 17 years old.

"This is one I will probably always remember," said Venus of the win. "I can say this is where it all started."

The singles win wasn't the end of Venus's success in Oklahoma City. Thirty minutes after winning the singles title, Venus teamed up with Serena to win the doubles final as well. It was the Williams sisters' first win as a team.

According to Venus, playing doubles with Serena is a lot of fun.

"I love playing doubles with Serena," Venus has said. "No matter what, we always have fun. Whenever we get too serious, we say to each other, 'Do you remember last year when we were playing at Indian Wells, we were losing, we were no good. How we laughed even though we were losing?'"

1998 Lipton Championships

After battling it out with both the Williams sisters at the Lipton Championships in 1998, Martina Hingis said, "Things are changing pretty quickly in tennis. Before, I was the hunter, and now I am the hunted one. This position is very different."

Lipton is considered the most important women's tournament after the Grand Slams. So when Venus blasted her way through the opening rounds without losing a single set, it showed that her game was maturing.

Serena did well too. She advanced to the quarterfinals, but there she lost to Hingis. This set up a semifinal match between Venus and Hingis.

When Martina Hingis loses control of a game and is unable to score any points, she often loses emotional control. She has been known to throw temper tantrums and stalk off the courts sobbing. So when she lost the first nine of eleven games to Venus at Lipton, the audience must have been waiting for Hingis to lose control. The high emotions at tennis tournaments are part of the excitement.

This time, however, Hingis didn't lose it. She kept a smile pasted on her face, maybe because she wanted to make it less obvious that the situation was shifting, that she was no longer alone at the top.

Venus used her fast serves and strong groundstrokes to overcome Hingis. Some of her serves were as fast as 122 mph (196 km/h), a full 12 mph (19 km/h) faster than the next fastest server at Lipton that year (the next fastest just happened to be Serena).

To put the power of Venus's serve into perspective, among the men's players at Lipton in 1998, only 15 of the 96 were serving faster than Venus was. (Male players tend to be stronger; at the 2000 Australian Open, Andre Agassi smacked one serve at 199 mph [320 km/h].)

"When Venus is 19, her average serve is going to be 130 miles an hour [210 km/h]," Richard Williams predicted. "When Venus is 20? And her whole body fills in? And she's playing serve-and-volley? Boy, I'm going to feel sorry for those other girls."

Hingis used time-out tactics in both matches against the Williams sisters. She asked for medical attention for leg cramps while playing Serena. Then she was able to turn things around and beat Serena. Hingis also took a time-out while playing against Venus, this time asking to go to the bathroom late in the match. But Venus prevailed despite the break in concentration, defeating Hingis 6-2, 5-7, 6-2.

Hingis told reporters that she lost to Venus because she was tired at Lipton. But if she was tired, it wasn't from playing tennis. She hadn't played at all the day before, and the week before Lipton she had not been in a tournament.

"The pressure of being number one has drained the living hell out of Hingis," Richard Williams told *Sports Illustrated* in the spring of 1998. "I've told Venus, 'Nineteen ninety-eight is your year to take the number one spot.' But, as sad as this sounds, I kind of hope she doesn't take it this year. These girls, when they become number 1, they look older, they act older, they get tired fast. It's the pressure."

After winning the match against Hingis, Venus laughed with reporters, saying, "Serena gave me one pointer that really helped me, which I will not disclose to y'all for fear that it will appear in the papers and over television."

Richard Williams had his own ideas about what Serena told her sister. "'Go out and kick butt,'" Richard said. "That was what she told her."

Hingis said after her loss, "I guess it's pretty difficult to play the Williams family two matches in a row. Venus definitely has more confidence now . . . She changes the pace instead of just hitting the ball as hard as she can. She mixes it up. That makes her a more dangerous player."

The game against Hingis had taken a lot out of Venus, who was having trouble with her left knee. Richard Williams told the press: "When she hugged me after beating Hingis, she said, 'My knee is really hurting me, Daddy. I have to go see the trainer.'"

Richard, who doesn't hide his contempt for the killing pressure to win in professional tennis, reportedly told Venus to quit the match against Hingis if she was in pain.

What was Venus's response to her father's advice?

"I can't give this tournament away," she said. "I have to play. Champions don't complain my leg is hurting or my feet hurt when the going gets tough. Champions never give up."

By beating Hingis, Venus made it to the finals of the Lipton tournament. In the finals at Lipton, Venus would take on Anna Kournikova, who was a year younger than Venus, but had so far shown great promise.

Kournikova tried to blunt Venus's power by slicing the ball, which would cause it to spin and drop and come off Venus's racket in unexpected ways. Venus showed the patience of a true champion in defeating Kournikova. In other words, she didn't rely entirely on her power. The experts had been saying all along that if Venus really wanted to do it right, she would have to develop a more rounded, less power-dependent game.

Although Kournikova managed to last three sets, she was no match for Venus's nerve-shattering serve, her incredible strength, and her long reach. Venus won the match 6-2, 4-6, 1-6, taking her second tournament.

The win at Lipton put Venus into the No. 10 spot in the rankings. It was a great accomplishment. Only six other players in recorded women's tennis history had managed to climb from outside the top 100 into the top 10 in less than a year. Hingis herself had not climbed so fast in the rankings.

"I have the No. 1 and No.2 players in the world," Richard said after Lipton. "When they meet in a finals, I'm going to ask them to let me sit in the umpire chair."

Venus won one more tournament in 1998. She might have won more, but her knee gave her trouble. She had to quit in the middle of a tournament in San Diego and cancel her appearance at the Canadian Open.

Still, Venus had a great year. She won her first singles event ever, and then went on to win two more for good measure. She made it to the quarterfinals of every one of the Grand Slam events, and managed to go one better at the U.S. Open, making it to the semis. In fact, Venus made it to the quarterfinals or better in every single event she played in 1998, save two. In six of the events she played in, she made it to the finals.

If Serena didn't do as well as her sister in '98, she at least had a respectable showing. She made it to the quarterfinals at six tournaments and to the semis at one.

In doubles play, the girls were very successful. Together, they won two doubles tournaments. With their respective male partners, they swept the Grand Slam events, Venus and Gimelstob taking two, and Serena and Mirnyi taking the other two.

The girls were doing well. Still, neither Venus nor Serena had won a Grand Slam singles title by the end of 1998. If either of the girls were going to manage a Grand Slam title before the turn of the century, they were going to have to do it in 1999.

Chapter Five

The Big Four, 1999

1999 Australian Open

If ever there was a tennis match where emotions were a factor, it was Venus's quarterfinal match at the first Grand Slam of 1999.

The tournament in Melbourne, Australia, saw Venus playing Lindsay Davenport, who, at the end of 1998, had dethroned Martina Hingis to become the No. 1 ranked player in the world.

Venus managed to keep up relatively well in the first set against Davenport, although in the end she lost, 6-4. But the second set didn't start out well. Venus had her serve broken right away.

In tennis, one player serves all the points in a game and then the other player serves all the points in the next game. When a player has the serve, it can be a great advantage, especially for someone as powerful as Venus. When Venus had her serve broken, it meant that Davenport won a game that Venus was serving. The score was 2-0 for Davenport.

At the beginning of the third game of the second set,

some of Venus's hair beads flew off during a rally. Both Venus and Serena wear beads in their hair, often hundreds and hundreds of them. When the beads came out of Venus's hair during her match against Davenport, the referee called a let, meaning the point had to be played over. The referee claimed that Venus's flying beads were a distraction for Davenport.

Venus played the point over and was on the verge of breaking Davenport's serve when more hair beads came off. According to the rules, the second time a player is in violation of a regulation, she loses a point.

Besides losing a point, Venus lost her cool. She had already argued with the ref when he called the let, but it was when she lost a point that Venus really got angry. Reacting to his argument that her beads had caused a disturbance, Venus yelled, "There's no disturbance! No one's being disturbed!"

Losing that point lost Venus the game, and it was a game she was playing on her serve. At that point, she was down three games in the second set.

She was on the verge of tears, arguing loudly as more of her beads fell onto the court. She tried to appeal the point, but the referee referred to the rule: if a piece of clothing flies off, a warning can be given, followed by the loss of a point if it happens again.

Beads had flown off Venus's head in the past, but no umpire had ever done anything about it. Ball retrievers had simply scooped the beads up and the game had continued. The whole thing was too much for Venus; she didn't win a single game in the second set, losing the match, 4-6, 0-6.

At the end of the game, Venus refused to shake the umpire's hand. The crowd booed, which gives some indication of the excitement the Williams sisters bring to tennis. The crowd may not have been happy with Venus's behavior at the Australian Open, but they were involved, they were emotional, and they were bound to come back for more tennis excitement. All this is good news for women's professional tennis.

"They are going to turn the sport around," IGA tournament director Sara Fornaciari told *Vogue* magazine. "They have personality. They are smart. They are mature. I have never seen anything like their media skills."

Their mother, Oracene, says the girls developed these skills as a result of their upbringing. They were always encouraged "to be themselves, not to have any inhibitions. You're not really having fun," Oracene pointed out, "if you're not being yourself."

When Venus appeared on Jay Leno's late-night talk show, she got a lot of laughs at Leno's expense. Leno told her, "You've got the PR game down. Whoa. You're gonna be huge."

Venus has great confidence and determination. She believes in herself and the course she is steering in life, just as her father believed in the unorthodox course he took his two youngest daughters along in bringing them into the world of professional tennis.

Venus's confidence was certainly shaken when she lost to Lindsay Davenport in the quarterfinals of the 1999 Australian Open, but her determination was still intact. When asked if she would continue wearing beads on court, she exclaimed, "Why should I have to change? I like my hair."

When reporters asked Davenport if the beads were actually a distraction, Davenport said, "You can hear them, and see them a little bit. I'm not going to say it's a total distraction, but it is a little annoying. It's just things flying in the air that you're not supposed to be seeing."

Venus countered: "I don't think it's a real distraction, I don't think the other player on the other side is able to see it. I think they're focusing on the ball."

While Venus was embroiled in controversy over her hair beads, Serena was already out of the Australian Open, having made it to the third round where she lost to Sandrine Testud 2-6, 6-2, 7-9.

1999 French Open

Venus made it to the fourth round of the French Open and Serena only made it to the third round. But the girls had a little more success playing as a team in the doubles tournament in Paris.

They made it to the final, where they had to play

Martina Hingis and Anna Kournikova. Hingis and Kournikova were considered a dangerous team, seeded second at the tournament to Venus and Serena's ninth.

The Williams won the first set 6-3 and were up 5-1 in the second, just points away from their first Grand Slam women's doubles title, when Hingis and Kournikova came back, somehow clawing their way to a win in the second set.

Hingis and Kournikova were winning 5-4 in the third set, one game away from winning the doubles crown, when the Williams sisters finally decided it was time to turn things around. They fought back to 6-5 before it started to rain.

When it rains during an outdoor tennis match, the play is delayed until the rain stops. This was the second rain delay during the finals of the French Open doubles tournament. There was some fear that the rain delays were messing with the Williams sisters' concentration. But it seems these fears were unnecessary. The girls came back after the rain stopped and won their first Grand Slam doubles tournament.

"We should have finished it off in two," said Serena after the match was over. "That was devastating, we had match point. That definitely wasn't the way to go. We should have stayed calm and made our shots. We just got too tense and didn't perform."

1999 Wimbledon

At Wimbledon, Venus made it to the quarterfinals but lost to Steffi Graf, 2-6, 6-3, 4-6. Serena was sick and did not even play.

The girls would have one last chance to take a Grand Slam in the 20th century, and if past performance was any indication, it was going to be up to Venus, who had out-performed her sister at every Grand Slam event so far in 1999.

But past performance isn't always a good measure of who will prevail in future matches. Women's tennis became exciting during the last years of the 20th century because it was never predictable. There were always surprises, and the 1999 U.S. Open was to provide one of the most surprising finishes in recent years.

Chapter Six

The Last Grand Slam
of the Millennium

Coming into the 1999 U.S. Open, Serena was seeded seventh, meaning, basically, that she was considered the seventh most dangerous player at the tournament. There were six players considered more likely to win the U.S. Open, one of them being Serena's own sister, Venus

Serena had injured her shoulder a few weeks before the U.S. Open, but she was still able to play tennis and she decided she wanted to enter the tournament.

The U.S. Open is the final Grand Slam event of the year. Every player wants to win a Grand Slam (or two or three or ten), and this one was in Serena's home country.

Serena hadn't fared well in the other three Grand Slam events in 1999. She didn't get past the third round in either the French or Australian Open. She missed Wimbledon altogether after coming down with the flu.

Even after Serena stormed through the first and second rounds of the 1999 U.S. Open without losing a set, there was little reason to think she might go any further. She'd made it to the third round, but it was the third round that tripped her up in both the French and Australian Opens.

At the U.S. Open, the third round saw Serena go up against a player named Kim Clijsters. Although Belgium's Clijsters took the first set, 6-4, she was no match for Serena, who ultimately beat Clijsters to advance to the fourth round.

In the fourth round, Serena again lost the first set, 4-6, she went on to beat Spain's Conchita Martinez to move into the quarterfinals.

The quarterfinals saw Serena meet another veteran, an even stronger player than Martinez. Monica Seles was ranked world No. 4 when she met Serena on the courts at the Arthur Ashe Stadium in New York. Seles was 25 years old and had been playing professional tennis since she was 15. She dominated women's tennis in the early 1990s, and had won forty-four singles titles over the course of her ten-year career, nine of them at Grand Slam events.

Seles played hard, defeating Serena in the first set, 6-4, but it turned out that Seles had reached the peak of her performance. Once again, Serena put the juice on for the second and third sets, overwhelming Seles, 6-3 and 6-2.

Serena had made it to the semi-finals of the 1999 U.S. Open. Would she be able to match her sister's performance of two years earlier, when Venus had made it to the finals?

In the semi-finals, Serena came up against her toughest competition yet. Lindsay Davenport began playing tennis at the age of seven, about the time most kids are entering grade two. Seven might seem like a young age to be starting tennis, but compared to many of the players Davenport competes against, seven is at least two or three years too late.

Martina Hingis, for example, was holding a tennis racket when she was two or three years old. Venus and Serena Williams started playing tennis as preschoolers. The fact that Lindsay Davenport had started so late, yet was still able to take women's professional tennis by storm, is an indication of just how talented an athlete she is.

It is not terribly surprising that Davenport took to tennis so quickly, considering the athletic family she comes from. Her father participated in the 1968 Olympics and her mother and sisters play volleyball.

A week after turning professional in 1993, Lindsay Davenport upset the No. 5 ranked player in the world, Gabriela Sabatini. Not long after that, Davenport won her first major tour event, the 1993 European Open, and shot up in the rankings to No. 25. A year and a few months later, she was in the top 10.

At the 1996 Olympics, Davenport was seeded ninth, meaning she was considered the ninth most likely to win the gold medal. She beat No. 3 Arantxa Sanchez Vicario, No. 4 Iva Majoli, No. 5 Anke Huber, and No. 7 Mary Joe Fernandez to win the gold.

If Lindsay Davenport looked like a contender for world No. 1 at the beginning of her professional career, she didn't disappoint. In 1998 she was named Chase Player of the Month a record three straight months. She took her first Grand Slam singles event, the 1998 U.S. Open, on her mother's birthday. At the end of 1998, Davenport was ranked world No. 1, having toppled Martina Hingis, who had held onto the top spot for 80 weeks before Davenport took over.

Davenport lost the first set to Serena, 6-4, but it looked like she would dominate the rest of the match when she slaughtered Serena 6-1 in the second set. The final set was a fairly close one, but Serena took it 6-4 to advance to the finals, where she would face the number one seed, Martina Hingis.

In some ways, it was Martina Hingis's worst Williams sisters nightmare. Coming into the 1999 U.S. Open finals, she had just finished playing a tough semi-final match against Venus. Venus had fought hard, but had wound up losing to Hingis, thus losing any hope of winning a Slam in the 20th century.

What was more, if Serena took a Grand Slam before her older sister, Venus might have trouble recovering from the psychological blow.

Hingis went down in the first set of the finals, 6-3.

But the second set proved to be about as exciting as tennis can get. Hingis was down again, 5-3, and it looked like Serena would wrap it up with two match points to her favor. But Hingis fought back to force the game to a tiebreaker.

Serena had won all five tiebreakers she'd played so far in 1999. Sure enough, in this one she came on strong, immediately pulling ahead 3-1. But Hingis came back to make it 4 each. Serena went ahead 5-4 when she smashed Hingis's serve down the line, then took the next two points. When she saw Hingis's final shot drift long and land outside the court, Serena's knees buckled, and she cried, "Oh my God." She had won the tiebreaker.

Serena Williams was the 1999 U.S. Open Grand Slam champion. She had managed to grab a Grand Slam ahead of her sister and she had done it at the age of 17, just two years into her professional career.

Serena had beat Martina Hingis at her own game. Hingis, who is only a year or so older than Serena, has had an incredible career so far, winning five Grand Slam events and numerous other titles. She is a supreme all-court player, meaning she is strong in all areas, including her mental game. She serves well (although she has nothing of the powerful Williams sisters' speed), she can play the net, and she can play from the back of the court, making what are called baseline shots. Some commentators have likened

Hingis to a gymnast or a dancer because of her grace on court.

This time it was Serena who was likened to a gymnast, playing an all-around great game. While Hingis was unable to score a single ace, Serena got 8, putting her tournament total at 62, 40 more than any other player at the U.S. Open in 1999, including her sister who generally has more power in her serve.

But more important, Serena moved around the court quickly, played well at the net, and won many of the baseline rallies that went down throughout the match.

Serena's win at the U.S. Open made history on a number of counts. With fellow American Andre Agassi taking the men's title, it was the first time in nearly two decades that Americans had made a clean sweep of the U.S. Open singles titles.

Serena became the first black woman to win a Grand Slam event since Althea Gibson did it more than 40 years earlier in 1958. Sister Venus had won six singles events, but had yet to win a Slam.

Emotionally, the win was the highlight of Serena's career. "I didn't know what to do — laugh or cry or just scream — so I think I did it all."

For Venus Williams, the results of the U.S. Open were another story. Reporters described the look on Venus's face when she saw her sister win as one of envy. Even Serena commented on her sister's appearance: "I've never seen her that down before."

But whatever Venus felt, she and Serena went on to compete in the doubles event at the tournament, which they won to give them their second doubles Grand Slam. The Williams sisters now had seven Grand Slam trophies between them, including doubles, mixed doubles, and now Serena's singles win.

Between the two girls, the Williams family took home $1,290,000 of the U.S. Open purse. Serena took home $750,000 for the singles win; Venus got $210,000 for making the semi-finals. The doubles tournament paid the girls $330,000 to split between them.

Serena had a lot of messages on her cell phone after winning the U.S. Open, but there was one call she took immediately. The President of the United States, Bill Clinton, called. Clinton was in New Zealand where he was meeting with Asia-Pacific leaders.

"So, you follow tennis? I never knew," Williams said. "I'm glad you guys were watching. I hope you guys were cheering for me. If not, that's okay."

The President assured her he was rooting for her.

"Wow," was all Serena could manage.

After congratulating her on winning the Open, Clinton handed the phone over to his teenage daughter, Chelsea, so she could congratulate Serena.

Chelsea, a 19-year-old university student at the time, said she would show Serena around the campus of Stanford University the following week, since Serena was scheduled to play in a tournament there.

"Sure, if I'm around," Serena said, but quickly added, "I'm sure I'll be around."

When the two talked about Chelsea's major, History, Serena said, "That's definitely a tough subject. I don't think I would be able to do that. I excel in athletics."

"You most certainly do," was Chelsea's reply.

Chelsea's wasn't the only invitation. President Clinton also invited Serena, along with her entire family, to visit the White House for a personal tour. "Wow, I'm so excited," replied Serena. "We're definitely going to make a trip this year.

"I thought for sure my day couldn't get any better," Serena said after her presidential phone conversation. "And then I hear that the president wants to call. Pretty stoked."

At the end of the millennium, Venus and Serena were side by side in the rankings, No. 3 and No. 4 respectively. The only obstacles to taking the top spots were Martina Hingis and Lindsay Davenport.

"It's really amazing; I was always the one who said, 'I want to win the U.S. Open,' and Venus, she always wanted Wimbledon," said Serena.

In the end, what is needed to win out there is a combination of all the right factors. In terms of the mental game, a huge amount of concentration is needed along with quick thinking and the ability to anticipate what your opponent will do next. Physically, a player must be in top condition, with no injuries.

Above all, however, it takes an all-around strong game of tennis and Serena showed that she was able to play a very mature game when she met Hingis in the finals of the 1999 U.S. Open. It was tennis at its best, with both teens playing brilliantly. And it was a testament to Serena's maturing talent that she won a match filled with every imaginable tennis shot, showing the kind of court sense that only the greatest of the great can generally achieve.

Chapter Seven

Making History

Venus and Serena Williams are good for women's tennis. They bring new fans to the sport. More fans means more sponsors, and more sponsors means more money. Tennis, like other professional sports, is big business.

During the 1999 U.S. Open final between Serena and Martina Hingis, nearly six million households tuned in to watch the match on TV. Sixteen percent of all televisions turned on in the U.S. were tuned to the Open. This was an increase of 92 percent over the previous year. It was the highest-rated women's final since 1993.

The Grand Slam events may draw the most attention among tennis fans, but Venus and Serena saw a great deal of success in other tournaments they played in 1999.

Most often, if you see one of the Williams sisters at a tournament, the other one won't be far behind. But the Women's Tennis Association often holds two events at the same time in different parts of the world. In February of 1999, while Serena was in Paris playing in the Open Gaz de France, Venus was in Oklahoma City, in the U.S., playing in the tournament that she had won the year before, the IGA Classic.

At the Open Gaz, Serena powered her way through four rounds of tennis without losing a single set. This got her into the finals, where she did finally lose one set, but managed to prevail in the other two, winning the first singles tournament of her career.

Meanwhile, on the same day, February 28, Venus was in Oklahoma City playing in the finals of the IGA Superthrift Tennis Classic. Because of the time difference, Venus knew about Serena's win before she went onto the courts to play her match.

"I really felt that it was my duty to come out here and win," she told reporters. True to her word, Venus defended her title in Oklahoma City.

It was a day of celebration for the Williams family, but it was also a day for the history books. Venus and Serena were the first sisters in history to win tournaments on the same weekend.

When Richard Williams learned that his daughters had both won their tournaments he was overwhelmed: "This is just unreal. To have them both win brought tears to my eyes."

Serena went on to win her second tournament in a row, the Evert Cup, and then made it to the finals of the next tournament, the Lipton Championships. But the competition in the Lipton finals proved too much.

1999 Lipton Championships

Serena is shorter than her sister, but she is also more muscular. She sometimes gets whistled at by the boys when she takes off her warm-up jacket and reveals her sculpted shoulders.

Despite her incredible muscles, though, Serena's serve is less powerful than her sister's, mainly because Serena doesn't have Venus's height advantage.

At nearly 6'2" (188 cm), Venus has broken all the women's service records. At Zurich, Switzerland, in 1998 she slammed her fastest serve ever at 127.4 mph (205 km/h). This sizzling serve came at match point in a game against top French player Mary Pierce and was one of 13 service aces Venus blistered at Pierce during the match — 13 serves that Pierce did not even manage to get her racket on.

Although Serena is no slouch in the service department, her less powerful serve was definitely one of the factors in determining who would take the Lipton title in 1999.

Venus came to Lipton as the defending champion, having won the tournament the year before. She defended her title magnificently, getting to the finals by beating poor Steffi Graf, who no doubt had had enough of the Williams sisters after losing to Serena only recently at Indian Wells.

Serena also played well at Lipton, beating top-ranked players like Monica Seles, Amanda Coetzer, and, in the semi-finals, Martina Hingis. And so it was that, for the first time, the two Williams sisters met in the finals of a professional match.

It was, in fact, the first time sisters had met in any women's finals match in 115 years. The only other time it happened was in 1884 when Maud and Lilian Watson battled it out at Wimbledon.

In the historic match, Venus held off the younger Williams to take the Lipton Championships for the second year in a row. She beat Serena 6-1, 4-6, 6-4, in a match that took nearly two hours.

According to some commentators, it was apparent that neither of the Williams sisters was playing with the zest and cockiness they generally bring to the court.

Rick Macci, who has coached both girls, suggested that Serena has a great deal of respect for her older sister and would be nervous about defeating her. Venus, on the other hand, is determined that her little sister will not beat her. Venus kept her cool throughout the historic meeting, while Serena tossed her racket a few times after making errors.

After the match, the sisters hugged solemnly and left the court together, Venus with her arm around her little sister.

The media, hungry for sensation, like to play up the sibling rivalry angle when reporting on Venus and Serena, but the sisters seem content to go home together and forget the game once the result has been achieved.

Venus and Serena's father, Richard, on the other hand, seems determined to stir up a little action, if not outright trouble. Richard manages to get himself into the news almost as much as his girls. Since the Lipton was the first time the two had met in a final, Richard obviously felt he better make the most of it.

During the tournament, Richard held up a big sign that said, "WELCOME TO THE WILLIAMS SHOW." Who could blame him? No matter who won, seeing the sisters play against each other in a final was the culmination of a dream Richard Williams had hatched years earlier when he first started taking Venus and Serena to the glass-littered tennis courts in South Central LA

"I really thought I was going to cry," said Richard. "What was going through my mind was all the problems we've had in tennis, bringing the girls up, how difficult it was, the gang members, all the people out there. I was saying, 'Look where you are today.' It was so difficult for me to believe it."

While Richard was emotional, Venus and Serena shrugged off all the talk of sibling rivalry.

"It's not too big," Venus said. "In the end, we go home and live life. You have to be happy after that. You have to remind yourself it's a game and there's only one winner. Next week, there will be another opportunity."

If you listen to Serena, there is no sibling rivalry because when the two are playing together, they don't think of each other as sisters.

"I looked over at her sometimes, and I didn't consider her Venus or my sister," Serena told *USA Today*. "I just considered her an opponent."

Venus added, "There's great satisfaction [in defeating Serena] because she takes players down left and right. So to survive such an onslaught is great.

"It's tough when you lose in the finals," Venus continued. "Serena wanted to win. She always wants to win. That's her personality."

When asked if Serena would make a comeback, Venus exclaimed, "Serena always comes back."

Serena, who had won 16 straight matches before coming up against Venus in the Lipton finals, said she hadn't played that well.

Richard Williams agreed: "Serena might have been a little emotional at first. She has a tendency to feel out her opponent as she goes along. She tends to do like a big train. Run right over them. But I think she was out of it today."

The 1999 Lipton Championships would not be the last time these dynamic siblings faced each other on the tennis courts. "I definitely look forward to another final with Venus," Serena told reporters after the tournament. "It's what we always dreamed of."

Venus went on to win a number of other tournaments in 1999. She also lost a few. Besides the U.S. Open, where she watched her little sister beat her to the punch, winning the first Williams sisters' singles Grand Slam event, Venus also lost to Serena in the finals of the Grand Slam Cup in Germany.

It could not have been easy for Venus to see her little sister win the U.S. Open. On the one hand, she should have been happy that her best friend and constant companion had won a Grand Slam event. On the other hand, it certainly seemed to have broken her spirit not being the first Williams sister to win a Slam.

To have Serena beat her to the finals of the Grand Slam Cup must have felt like the last straw in some ways. But Venus showed her characteristic determination and went on to play to the utmost of her talent in the remaining tournaments of 1999.

1999 Swisscom Challenge

The Swisscom Challenge is held in Martina Hingis's home, Switzerland. Both Hingis and Venus were playing in the event. Hingis was seeded No. 1, Venus No. 2.

But before Venus could meet Hingis in a match, she had to play Irina Spirlea in the second round of the tournament. The media, always hungry for sensational stories, were quick to remind people that Irina was the woman who had bumped Venus during the 1997 U.S. Open and was fined for swearing during a postgame interview.

Much to the delight of spectators and members of the press present at the Swisscom Challenge, the animosity between the two players was rekindled when Williams, while leading 6-3, 5-1, began to do some stretches on the court as Spirlea prepared to serve.

After stretching out her hamstring, Williams did a set of splits, which brought the spectators to a great chorus of applause. Venus's antics were about the most exciting part of the match, which saw the American trounce her Romanian opponent in under an hour.

Spirlea, not one to be outdone, imitated Venus, doing some exaggerated leg stretches herself, which got the crowd even more worked up. After the tournament, Venus shrugged the incident off.

"My hamstrings were feeling tired," she told reporters, "so I had to loosen the muscles."

Venus then went on to the quarterfinals of the tournament where she blew sixth-seeded Julie Halard-Decugis of France away, beating her 6-2, 6-3. In the semi-finals she took on another French woman, third seed Mary Pierce, defeating her 6-4, 6-4.

Six thousand fans packed into the Kloten sports hall to witness Venus and Martina Hingis battle it out in the finals of the Swisscom Challenge.

Venus needed to win. She had met Hingis twelve times and beaten her four, but she had never been able to take her down in a final. If she could not beat

Hingis in a final, where the pressure to win was at its greatest, her chances of becoming No. 1 were slim.

Hingis was playing with some advantages. Her mother, who was also her coach, was there at courtside to cheer her on, whereas Venus was alone; for the first time ever, she was at a tournament without her mother, father, or sister Serena.

Hingis had another important advantage. She was on home soil in Switzerland. The sellout crowd of fans was there to see Martina. When their national hero broke Venus's serve and moved ahead in the first set 2-0, the crowd went crazy.

Perhaps Hingis was too set on winning at home. She had tried so hard, playing in the tournament four previous times, but only making it past the quarterfinals once. Here she was in the finals, her big chance, and she had to defeat one of the toughest players on the circuit, who was also her biggest rival.

Venus decided it was her day. "It's all about taking advantage of opportunities," she said after the tournament, "and today I took them."

A year before at Swisscom, Venus had made it to the finals but had lost to Lindsay Davenport, even though she blasted one record-breaking ace of 127 mph (204 km/h) during the tournament.

This year, Venus was determined not to repeat history. After Hingis broke Venus's serve, Venus came right back and broke Hingis's serve. Then she kept

Hingis stuck in the backcourt to break her serve twice more, taking the first set, 6-3.

By the second set, Hingis seemed unhinged. Venus continued to pummel her and went ahead 4-2, after once again breaking her serve. Hingis broke back, giving the crowd a reason to cheer. But Venus came back, winning the second set 6-4, which won her the tournament.

"I had my chances, especially in the second," said a weary Hingis. "She was just playing the last shot better. I'm not really disappointed because I feel if I work on my conditioning I can beat her again. The tennis season is long and to stay on top mentally all year long is difficult."

Venus had finally accomplished what she needed to do, if only for the sake of her confidence. She had beaten the world No. 1 player in a final. And to make the victory sweeter, she had done it on her opponent's home soil. Throughout the entire Swisscom tournament, Venus had not lost a single set.

Since neither her mother nor her father were in Switzerland with her, Venus had to celebrate with the only member of the family who came along — her dog, Pete (named after men's tennis great Pete Sampras).

"I was a bit sad," said Williams. "I felt a little bit incomplete. Before the match I wanted to talk to [my parents] but with the time difference I couldn't reach them and I had to leave a message on the machine. I was glad to see I could play well even if they aren't here.

"It's like I want to run home and say, 'Mom, Dad, look what I did.' Naturally, as you get older you have to do things on your own . . . that's the way life is. But I would love to have them with me."

Venus lost in the semi-finals of the last two tournaments she played in 1999, but the Williams sisters had made their mark. Even if neither of them ever played another game of professional tennis in their lives, they would be remembered.

Chapter Eight

Moving On

Serena Williams turned pro in October 1997 and entered the women's circuit rankings at number 453. Before the year was out, she was ranked as one of the hundred best players on the women's circuit. In one tournament alone, in Chicago, she jumped from No. 304 to No. 102.

At the same tournament in Chicago, Serena set a record by becoming the lowest ranked player ever to beat two top 10 players in a single championship. She beat No. 7 Mary Pierce in the second round of a tournament, and she beat No. 4 Monica Seles in the quarterfinals. It was only the fifth tournament of her professional career — her 13th and 14th career matches.

Within three months, Serena was into the top 50, and by June 1998 she was into the top 20. Two years after she turned professional, Serena Williams was ranked No. 4 in the world, one place behind her sister, with only Lindsay Davenport and Martina Hingis ahead of the two Williams sisters.

Venus climbed in the rankings at a similarly rapid

rate. When she played at Indian Wells, California in 1997, she was ranked No. 211. By the time she got to the season-ending Grand Slam event, the 1997 U.S. Open, she was ranked No. 66. When the U.S. Open was done, Venus was ranked No. 27. Less than a year later, by the middle of the 1998 season, Venus was No. 5. By the end of 1999, she was No. 3.

Both girls have won a number of awards, and in fact the Williams family held the WTA Tour Most Impressive Newcomer award two years in a row, Venus taking it in 1997 and Serena in 1998.

But the Williams sisters' incredible talent accounts only partially for the fascination with them among fans and members of the press. What really makes the girls so interesting is the personality each brings to the game.

They are like other teenage girls in many ways, going to the mall, shopping, and talking about boys. In the world of professional tennis, however, the girls are unusual — a pair of extremely self-possessed, well-educated, family-oriented girls in an environment that often strains family relations and can leave young women with emotional problems.

Richard Williams has constantly criticized the women's tennis establishment as amoral — without values — yet he has thrust his girls into this world and made wild predictions about their future success.

At the same time, both Richard and Oracene have

provided their daughters with a religious grounding that has made Venus and Serena remarkably sure of themselves in a world where teenagers often have trouble coping.

Venus is perhaps more emotionally controlled than her sister. Serena, it has been said, tends to go from one emotional extreme to another, charming fans and the press one moment, acting aloof and haughty the next. But both girls have incredible confidence.

It is sometimes difficult to talk about one of the Williams sisters without talking about the other. They seem to be together constantly. They practice together, they travel to tournaments together, and they shop and dine together.

Past tennis professional Pam Shriver, who has been Venus's mentor, says the girls are "best friends, doubles partners, practice partners." She claims that tennis has never seen two players this close, particularly not two who were ranked in the top 10.

Venus and Serena are almost always profiled together by the media. Their approaches to the game of tennis are constantly compared, so much so that they get sick of talking about each other. In an interview before the Family Circle Cup tournament in the spring of 1999, Serena was asked to compare her style of tennis to that of her sister.

"Venus has a bigger serve," she started to say. "I don't know. It's kind of hard to say . . . of course there are differences. I really don't want to talk about it. It's so boring."

Serena hasn't always been so reluctant to compare her own game to that of her sister. She has, in the past, said that she considers Venus a role model, but that she also watches to see what mistakes Venus makes and tries not to make the same mistakes herself.

Talking about Venus's appearance at the 1997 French Open, Serena said, "She did a lot of crazy things, like she wasn't able to close out her second-round match. I was able to see the things she did and not make the same mistakes."

Venus and Serena's self-confidence borders on arrogance at times. Sally Jenkins of *Women's Sports and Fitness* magazine interviewed the girls at the end of 1998 and found them blunt to the point of being rude. Before Jenkins had a chance to ask a single question, Serena said, "This is preposterous," and began to walk away. Her mother called her back.

Jenkins tried asking a number of questions, but the girls were completely unresponsive. Finally, in desperation, she asked what Venus and Serena would like to talk about.

"I don't want to talk about my hair," Venus said.

"Very boring," Serena agreed.

Of course, they have talked to reporters about their hair in the past, numerous times, but obviously, after a time, any topic of conversation will get boring if it's overdone. It's the same with signing autographs, which Venus has claimed can be a real drag. It's the same with anything, really, and one wonders how long it will be before the girls get bored with tennis.

Richard Williams has indicated on a number of occasions that he is surprised his two youngest daughters are still in the game.

"Tennis is a good way to make a million dollars," he told *Jet* magazine in 1998. "But they've done that already, and then some. They're so brilliant, they'll be great in anything they do."

The unwavering support they get from their parents has no doubt helped Venus and Serena achieve such overwhelming success. The two are not hesitant in praising their parents. In 1998, Serena told *Newsweek* magazine: "My dad means everything to me, because he really brought me up, gave me life and supported me through all the years."

Sometimes the family connection gets downright weird, especially if you listen to Richard, who can be a bit unconventional at the best of times.

"I really don't want them to have friends outside the family," Richard has said. "Jennifer Capriati had friends, and that's how she got messed up. They have each other. That's all they need."

The girls have embraced their parents' religion; both are devout Jehovah's Witnesses. "Lots of people don't know much about it, so they have a prejudice about it," Venus has said about her religion. "We make sure that whatever we do is in line with what God would want us to do."

The girls attend the Kingdom Hall for Jehovah's Witnesses three times a week. Even when they are on the road, they hunt down the local Hall and attend services. At home, when they are not playing tennis or shopping at the mall, they sometimes go door to door, preaching their religion.

Both girls have worked hard and done well at school, and both have made plans for their lives after their tennis careers. This is important, since most professional tennis players don't continue playing much past the age of 30. Serena has said she would like to be a veterinarian and Venus has repeatedly claimed she would like to design clothing.

Serena has said of her relationship with her sister, "We're totally different people with different hearts. I've always believed that I can be the best, and I'm sure she believes the same thing about herself."

Around the time of the 1999 U.S. Open, word had it that Venus and Serena were getting ready to move out of the family home. They had purchased 10 acres of land near their parents' house. They paid a half million dollars and were planning to have a house built. They were leaving the nest. But they weren't going far, and they certainly weren't leaving each other.

As for tennis, Venus and Serena are really only beginning their careers. How will they do in the 21st century? Will they continue to succeed? Will Serena continue to outpace her older sister? Will they continue to play tennis at all?

Venus did not play any games between November 1999 and April 2000 due to tendinitis — a painful inflammation — in her wrists. In March 2000, Richard Williams told reporters that his daughter was already considering retirement at the ripe old age of 19. But Venus herself made no official announcement.

Meanwhile, Serena's performance at the 2000 Australian Open was lackluster. She didn't even make it to the quarterfinals. She seemed almost relieved to be out of the tournament, telling reporters she had a lot of homework, including 38 drawings to complete for a design course she was doing.

Only time will tell where the girls' lives will lead them. One thing, however, is certain: Venus and Serena have changed the world of women's tennis. They have brought a whole new audience to the game. They have acted as role models for young African Americans.

Venus and Serena may forget the world of tennis sooner than their fans would like, but the world of tennis will not soon forget Venus and Serena Williams.

Glossary of Tennis Terms

ace: A serve in which the opponent is unable to touch or barely touches the ball as it flies past.

backhand: A stroke from the side of the body opposite the side the player normally serves from. When a player uses both hands on the racket to hit a backhand, it is called a **two-handed backhand**.

baseline shot: A shot made from the back of the court, near the baseline, usually after the ball has bounced once in the court.

court: Area on which tennis is played. Tennis courts can be made of any one of several different surfaces, including asphalt, concrete, carpet, clay, or grass.

crosscourt: A shot that travels diagonally across the tennis court.

deuce: Term for the score in a tennis game that is tied.

drop shot: A shot that is generally hit very softly and is aimed to drop just on the other side of the net. Tends to be used when the opponent is at the baseline and will have to run to try to get the ball.

fault: Error made when a player serves and the ball hits the net, or is out of bounds when it lands in the opponent's court. When a player steps on or over the baseline while serving, it is called a **foot fault**. For each point, a player gets two chances to serve; if she faults both times, it is called a **double fault** and she loses the point.

game: The smallest division of a tennis match. Once one of the players has scored four points, the first player to be two points ahead wins a game.

Grand Slam: The winning of all four of the major tennis tournaments in a row: the Australian Open, the French Open, Wimbledon, and the U.S. Open. Each of the above four events is sometimes described as a Grand Slam.

ground stroke: Any shot a player uses to hit the ball back after it has bounced once on her side of the court. If the ball lands in the player's court and she is unable to get it before it bounces a second time, that player loses the point.

lob: A shot hit high in the air so as to go over the head of the opponent, but still land in bounds. Generally used when the opponent is close to the net.

love: Term used when a player has no points in a game.

majors: The four most important tennis championships each year: the Australian Open, the French Open, Wimbledon, and the U.S. Open. Sometimes called the **Big Four**, or Grand Slam events. If a player wins all four in a row, she has won a Grand Slam.

match: The full tennis contest. In women's tennis, the first player to win two **sets** wins the match. The winner of a match goes on to play in the next round of a **tournament**.

point: The scoring element in tennis. The full point-scoring terminology for tennis is listed below:

> 0 points = love
>
> 1 point = 15
>
> 2 points = 30
>
> 3 points = 40
>
> 4 points = game (provided the player is ahead
> by two points)

If both players reach 40, they are said to be at **deuce**.

rally: The back and forth exchange of play that leads to one player winning a single point

seeding: A list of players ranked according to their past performance. Players who have done well in past tournaments are seeded higher than players who have not done so well in the past. The highest seeds at a tournament do not generally play each other in the early rounds. This keeps the stars in the tournament longer.

set: A division of a tennis match made up of a number of games. The first player to win six games and to be ahead by two, wins the set. If both players reach six games without either being ahead by two, a **tiebreaker** is played. The first player to win two games wins the **match**.

tiebreaker: A single game played when a set goes beyond six games and neither player is ahead by two. The winner of that game takes the set.

tournament: Large tennis competition, played on a round-robin basis. A player moves to the next round of the tournament when she has won a **match** (see above). The last player in the tournament, who has not lost a single match, wins the tournament.

volley: Hitting the ball before it has bounced on the court. Some players like to get up close to the net and hit the ball hard, at an angle that can make it impossible to return.

Women's Tennis Association (WTA): The association that represents professional women tennis players, supervises tournaments, and ranks the players according to a point scoring system that sees the best players at each tournament get the most points.

Research Sources

An interview with: Venus Williams (1998 State Farm Evert Cup, Indian Wells, California), http://www.asapsports.com/tennis/1998evert/031098VW.html, March 10, 1998

Bernard, Sarah, "Venus Rising: Teenage tennis superstar plays the hype game", *New York*, November 23, 1998, p. 17

Bodo, Peter, "Talk isn't cheap on the WTA Tour", *Tennis*, March 1998, p. 22

Bodo, Peter, "Open season on the slams", *Tennis*, June 1998, p. 48

Bricker Charles "Williams moves up in tennis rankings", www.sun-sentinel.com, March 14, 1997

Chappell, Kevin, "Venus goes for no. 1", *Ebony*, August 1998, p. 38

Chua-Eoan, Howard and Barovick, Harriet,"Her Serena Highness", *Time South Pacific*, September 20, 1999, p. 62

"Doing it alone: Venus Williams beats Hingis for Swisscom Challenge title", http://www.cnnsi.com/tennis/news/1999/10/17/hingis_venus/index.html, Sunday, October 17, 1999

Evans, Howie, "Venus continues her quest for no. 1 at $2 million Chase Championships", *New York Amsterdam News*, November 12, 1998, p. 50

———, "Venus defeats Serena in family showdown", *New York Amsterdam News*, April 1, 1999, p. 48

———, "Venus Williams gains top 10 with Lipton championship win", *New York Amsterdam News*, April 2, 1998, p. 52

———, "Venus wins first title as Tiger loses in playoff", *New York Amsterdam News*, March 3, 1998, p. 49

Evans, Howie, "Venus wipes out Pierce as she heads for the French Open", *New York Amsterdam News*, May 13, 1999, p. 48

Finn, Robin, "American Shutout: Chang is Ousted", The New York Times on the Web (http://www.nyt.com), May 31, 1998

————, "Little sister grows up: Serena Williams wins U.S. Open", The New York Times on the Web (http://www.nyt.com), September 12, 1999

Greene Bob, "Inside Tennis", *National Post*, October 14, 1999, p. B12

Hackett, Thomas, "The importance of being Irina", *Tennis*, September 1998, p. 76

Higdon, David, "Beyond Power", *Tennis*, February 1998, p. 26

Howard, Johnette, "Bragging Rights", *Tennis*, November 1999, p. 36

Jenkins, Sally, "Double Trouble", *Women's Sports and Fitness*, November/December 1998, p. 102

Jet, "Richard Williams, father of Venus and Serena, says he wishes his girls would quit tennis", September 21, 1998, p. 49

———, "Serena Eclipses Venus in Sister-to-Sister Showdown", October 18, 1999, p. 53

———, "Venus Williams Penalized After Beads Fall On Court; Loses In Australia Open Quarterfinal", February 15, 1999, p. 50

———, "Venus Williams Tops Sister Serena To Repeat As Lipton Champion", April 12, 1999, p. 52

———, "Venus Williams Victorious At Italian Open In Rome", May 24, 1999, p. 53

———, "Williams sisters display loving sibling rivalry at Australian Open", February 2, 1998, p. 49

———, "Williams Wins $800,000 In Grand Slam Cup", October 26, 1998, p. 50

Kamlet, Ken, "Going it alone", *Tennis*, September 1999, p. 37

Kirkpatrick, Curry, "Waiting, impatiently, for Venus to rise", *Newsweek*, September 12, 1994, p. 70

Leand, Andrea, "Mixing it up", *Tennis,* September 1998, p. 11

"Like, wow! It's the president" http://www.cnnsi.com/tennis/1999/us_open/news/1999/09/11/clinton_call_ap, September 11, 1999

"Little resistance: Hingis, Venus dominate at Swisscom Challenge", http://www.cnnsi.com/tennis/news/1999/10/14/swisscom_venus/, October 14, 1999

Montville, Leigh, "Slice girls: Serena and Venus Williams cut up some top foes — and did some cutting up themselves — in Australia", *Sports Illustrated,* February 2, 1998, p. 66

"No match: Graf ends superlative career at top of her sport", http://cnnsi.com/statitudes/timeline/news/1999/08/13/graf_retirement/, August 13, 1999

"Nothing left to prove: tearful Graf announces immediate retirement", http://cnnsi.com/tennis/news/1999/08/13/graf_retires_ap/index.html , August 14, 1999

Peyser, Marc and Samuels, Allison, "Sister Act: Venus and Serena Shake up Tennis; Venus and Serena against the world", *Newsweek,* August 24, 1998, p. 44

Price, S.L., "Father Knew Best", *Sports Illustrated,* September 20, 1999, p. 38

———, "In her long-delayed debut, Venus Williams couldn't live up to her own billing", *Sports Illustrated,* July 7, 1997, p. 26

———, "Venus envy", *Sports Illustrated,* September 15, 1997, p. 32

Reed Julia, "Sisters at court", *Vogue,* May 1998, p. 270

Rhoden, William C., "Davenport's special skill is patience", The New York Times on the Web (http://www.nyc.com), September 12, 1998

Rodman, Dennis, "The 20 most fascinating women in politics", *George,* September 1998, p. 110

Rutledge, Rachel, *The Best of theBest in Tennis (Women of Sports Series).* The Millbrook Press, Inc., Brookfield, Connecticut, 1998

Serena Williams 1997 Record, http://www.williamssisters.com/S97.htm

Serena 1998 Record, http://www.williamssisters.com/Ser.htm

Serena Williams 1999 win-loss record, http://www.cnnsi.com/tennis/stats/1999/news.serena99.html

"Serena's Super Saturday: Williams defeats Hingis for first Grand Slam title", http://www.cnnsi.com/tennis/1999/us_open/news/1999/09/11/women_final_ap/index.html, September 12, 1999

"Sister act: Williams duo defeats Hingis, Kournikova for doubles title",http://www.cnnsi.com/tennis/1999/french_open/news/1999/06/06/williams_doubles/index.html, October 14, 1999

"Smash sisters: Venus and Serena Williams are tearing up women's tennis with a style all their own", http://sikids.com/magazine/williams/index.html

"So long, Serena: Third-seeded Williams stunned by 16th-seeded Likhovtseva", http://www.cnnsi.com/tennis/2000/australian_open/news/2000/01/23/williams_monday_ap/, January 24, 2000

Tebbutt, Tom, "There's no gender equity found in these courts", *The Globe and Mail*, October 9, 1999, p. S4

"Teleconfernece Interview with Serena Williams", http://www.aesir.com/FamilyCircleCup/1999-Interviews/1999-swilliams.html

Tennis, "Court Chatter", September 1998, p. 19

"They love new York: Williams sisters capture women's doubles crown", http://www.cnnsi.com/tennis/1999/us_open/news/1999/09/12/williams_doubles/, September 12, 1999

Thomsen, Ian, "Changing of the guard", *Sports Illustrated*, April 6, 1998, p. 64

Time for Kids, "Tennis' Slammin' Sisters!", March 12, 1999, p. 2

"U.S Open Notebook: Serena racks up on Flushing-ware", http://www.cnnsi.com/tennis/1999/us_open/news/1999/09/12/open_notebook_ap/, September 13, 1999

"USTA celebrates Black History Month, Part IV: The Williams sis-

ters (Venus and Serena) and the future", http://www.usta
.com

Vecsey, George, "Venus' Mom Delivers Hard Truth", The New York Times on the Web (http://www.nyt.com), June 3, 1998

"Venus loses her glow: No. 1 seed Davenport wins noisy quarterfinal with Williams", http://www.cnnsi.com/tennis/1999/australian_open/news/1999/01/26/open_roundup/, Tuesday, January 26, 1999

Venus Williams 1994–1996 Record, http://www.williamssisters.com/V96.htm

Venus Williams 1998 win-loss record, http://www.cnnsi.com/tennis/stats/1998/news.williams98.html

Venus Williams 1999 win-loss record, http://www.cnnsi.com/tennis/stats/1999/news.venus99.html

"Volley ball: Venus Williams, Tauziat advance to quarterfinals", http://cnnsi.com/tennis/news/1999/11/11/advanta_thurs_ap/index.html, November 11, 1999

WTA tour players: Serena Williams, http://www.wtatour.com/players/w234.php3

WTA tour players: Venus Williams, http://www.wtatour.com/players/w220.php3

We hope you have enjoyed this
CHAMPION SPORT Biography.

We welcome your comments and suggestions.

Please contact us at

Warwick Publishing

162 John Street
Toronto, Ontario, Canada
M5V 2E5

Telephone: (416) 596-1555

FAX: (416) 596-1520

E-Mail: mbrooke@warwickgp.com

— • —

Please visit our Web site at

www.warwickgp.com